A

Quebec City

Boyhood

For Anna-Marie and Johnny
     —who made it possible,
and for Dan, Veste, Harold, Bernadette,
Maudie, Tom and Teresa,
     —who also have their stories.

A
Quebec City Boyhood

by

Joseph Griffin

Introduction by Marianna O'Gallagher

Borealis Press
Ottawa, Canada
2001

Canada

We acknowledge the financial support of the Government of
Canada through the Book Publishing Industry Development
Program (BPIDP), and the Canada Council
for our publishing activities.

Canadian Cataloguing in Publication Data

Griffin, Joseph, 1931-
  A Quebec City Boyhood

Poems.
ISBN 0-88887-274-7

  I. Title.

PS8563.R53513Q84 2001   C811".6 C2001-900018-9
PR9199.3.G765Q84 2001

Cover design by Bull's Eye Design, Ottawa, Canada.
Printed and bound in Canada on acid free paper

Acknowledgements

"Nanny Goat's Path," "St. Patrick Street, 1941,"
"War Games," and "Christian Brothers" first appeared
in *The Nashwaak Review.*

Cover photograph courtesy of Dan Griffin.

Contents

INTRODUCTION

Once upon a time, a long time ago, in my first year in university, I heard a wonderful professor discourse on the "poetry of the Bible." At the same time in another class I was agreeably subjected, seriously for the first time, to 20th century poetry, after years of high school mooning over the Romantic poets. My happy conclusion to the melding of the two classes in my head was that the Biblical prophets and the 20th century poets played the same role, spoke the same message; that is, they cast the same thoughtful eye upon their particular milieu and its mores and showed things that they saw which were invisible to their contemporaries. Later readers would realize that the poet and the prophet are the same.

All this to say that the poet today still carries out the role of making us fathom the past and its depth of pain and passion; or makes us savour again the events of the past nonetheless vivid for their distance in time. Nostalgia gives us ownership of our past. Does everyone wonder if children of today have as much fun, or such rich experiences "as we did?"

Joseph Griffin's poems, poetic essays, evoke an era, a space and a spirit that have almost disappeared. Quebec City in the period just before and during the Second World War had a vibrant cohesive Irish community centred around Saint Patrick's Church and Schools. Griffin's *Prologue* to *A Quebec City Boyhood* speaks the poet's vision, evidence we recognize.

Geographically, the main body of the Irish of Quebec lived in the Upper Town, the part today called the Plateau, where the schools and the church could be found. However, there was never an Irish ghetto—the Irish lived everywhere in the city and suburbs—but there were a few small areas of concentration: around the Parliament Buildings (one might remember Artillery, Berthelot, Burton, Michael, D'Artigny, St. Amable named Amiable Street by the Irish, and Lachevrotière of Joe's poem); Champlain Street or "the Cove." These and other streets outside the walls, in the western part of the city, still surrounded by the tramway belt line, compassed the major portion of the community. The new Saint Brigid's Home had moved from McMahon Street around 1860 to de Salaberry Avenue, and the prople living in the Montcalm Suburb had begun to go to Sunday Mass there and to have the sacraments bestowed upon them in the chapel. A new Saint Patrick's Church opened on Grande Allée around 1914 and the new boys' school opened nearby in 1918. The Plains of Abraham and the Cove Fields, Quebec City's wonderful greenbelt, became the playgrounds for the children of Saint Patrick's.

This Irish Catholic community stemmed from two early sources. Irish businessman and their families had settled in Quebec City as early as the 1790s, originally from Waterford and Wexford, Limerick and Galway, not surprising since these seaports were linked with Quebec. These were the men who had pioneered the creation of a national church within the city by 1832—Saint Patrick's. The other cohesive group was comprised of the descendants of those hardy men and women who had moved into the Cove immediately after their emigrant experience, had created a neighbourhood at the same time as they took on the task of loading the ships in the burgeoning years of the timber trade during the Napoleonic Wars. In addition to creating a flavourful neighbourhood, they had founded the first labour union in Canada: the Quebec Benevolent Shiplabourers Association.

ix

So, against this background several generations of Irish grew up owning the whole city, and owning their Irishness, too. Joe Griffin has captured, in low key, but in authentic lines what we lived. The actual place names used, and the events are there for local colour, but the universal human experience is there as well—growing up, feeling family relationships, learning personal needs, and realizing one's capacities, eye openers all.

I hope that readers will bring their own nostalgia to the book. I know that several generations of Quebecers will revel in, laugh and cry, at what Joe Griffin remembers and what he has preserved for us in these few telling lines.

Marianna O'Gallagher
Quebec, November 2000

PROLOGUE

RIGHTS OF WAY

Walking the streets of the old city
    D'Artigny, D'Auteuil, Dauphine
    Charlevoix, Couillard, Champlain
and naming the streets as his people had
as he'd heard them called as a boy
    Abraham Hill, Mountain Hill, Palace Hill
    Maple Avenue, John, Grand Alley
he knew then that the city
had been his city
as surely as to the country child
the daisy field, the sliding hill
the picnic tree were his.

Climbing the medianed boulevard
the one they ran over his old streets
    Julia, Michael, Lachevrotière
    Artillery, Saint-Cyrille, Plessis
(the ramparted city kept intact
the one without the walls
was deemed without a past)
he rued his loss as that country man
his tarred-under daisies, his levelled hill
his felled yew
all for a new recreational center
or to let the traffic through.

DE LACHEVROTIÈRE STREET

Memory strikes stone soon
before Lachevrotière:
they'd lived in *le quartier latin*
by the old university
on Couillard and Saint-Flavien
and he still saw
walking along the Ramparts
and in the mornings
the big boys streaming
towards *le petit seminaire*:
taxi-driver peaked caps
navy-blue long coats
with white piping
and wide green sashes
ends hanging almost to the knee.

Lachevrotière renders up
more of shape and sound:
second-floor flat
over straw-hatted
Rondeau's grocery store
bay window reaching out to
the Berthelot playground
(*Vive la canadienne* and *Al-ta-la*
ringing out summer long)
and the Zouave hall
where on summer Sunday mornings
they would skim off
with generous fingers

the top inches of vanilla ice cream
from huge milk cans outside
till the inner voice
or the fear of some outer one
drove them off to church or play.

Memory seizes too
without extracting whole
a narrative broken—
with pieces left behind.
There was a back gallery
and other tenants' galleries
looking into a dirt courtyard.
One day he'd heard or seen
an instance of spousal abuse:
a line of curses or
a blow struck clean
or glancing
upon the young wife
across the way or down below.
He'd seen his father gasp
told by his mother that he
a tot of five or six
would be called to witness
at the court.
As they approached the day
his father told him many times:
"Just say the truth, son
just say the truth."
The time arrived
he took the witness box.
The judge called

a huddle of black robes.
Then "Merci mon petit bonhomme"
and raising his head
"Il est trop jeune
pour être témoin."

The rest of life
on Lachevrotière
is mostly shards and shreds:
their Irish aunt
calling it Lashevletaire
their first watermelon
shared by the Boudreaus upstairs
the agonizing blare
of the Zouaves bugle band
the day the German shepherd
bit him on the thigh.
So memory will not suffice.
You need a tale
another device of mind
to bring to play upon the watermelon
Zouave's horn and shepherd's bite.
The habit of the brain
is to attire what's known.
The slanted truth you say
is straight
but in a larger way.

PATENT-LEATHER SHOES

They'd talk about it for weeks
before and afterwards
their battered feet soaking
in solutions of Epson salts
or bantering as they played at euchre.
It was always in July
the month of the Feast
and always at night:
down the hill and straight out
as far as the Anglo
then turn right
and you were on your way
twenty-one miles of two-lane blacktop
at first high above the St. Lawrence
the road bridging the Montmorency above the Falls
(unseen but mighty in its roar)
then gradually down to river level
and the long aching endless stretch
till you saw the twin unfinished towers
as dawn slipped into day.

He'd never done it himself
they'd never let him.
"You're too young," his father said.
"You'd never last. In a few years."
But he'd never done it.
He'd left town to go away to school
and when he returned as a young man
the vogue had all but ended.

But he had his own story
to tell about St. Anne's
and he remembered now
sitting with his distraught father
in the torrid dusty afternoon train
back to the city
his shoes off, his burning feet
finally eased after a morning's torture.
His father had bought them
the day before
haggling over the price probably
black patent-leather
pleasing him as only
new shoes can a small boy.

He knew right off that morning
when he squeezed into them
but it was pride that kept him going
and the shiny shoes themselves
and his father's buying them for him:
the walk from Joachim
down the hill to the station
the hour-long train ride
Mass in the bright vaulted Basilica
the climb up the stairs on their knees
in the White Nuns' chapel
the breakfast of bacon and eggs
his father savoured so
the visit to the Cyclorama
and as after an eternity
boarding the train for the trip home.

His father saw the tears then
and understood
and bid him remove the shoes.
"I'll take them back. It's okay.
We'll get you another pair.
Why didn't you tell me?"
then patting his back
"You're a hero, son."

The story went around
inside the family and beyond
and for a while he did feel a hero
at least among his elders.
In time the blisters healed
and he got another pair of Sunday shoes.
But he never heard them
boast about their walks again
but that he didn't think—
though they never let him
join them on their night-time trek—
he had as well as they
honored the Saint to whose shrine
they'd walked so far to pray.

NANNY GOAT'S PATH

Picnicing on the gently rolling part
of the Plains of Abraham
in sight of the Woman's Prison
with the Dawsons, his tiny sister
and younger brothers and his mother
(his father at home
sleeping off the 12 to 8 shift at the Arsenal)
the late-June day sunny and warm
the whim took him and
not measuring, as boys will
his eleven years against
her thirty-six
and her high heels
and her silk stockings
and her tight skirt
he invited his mother to go with him
down the Nanny Goat's Path
to the beach at L'Anse au foulon.

He knew the path too well himself
(in their own talk at least
the way Wolfe's soldiers
had come up the cliff the night before
the Battle of the Plains of Abraham)
had travelled it up and down
with his brothers and pals
to get to and from the beach—
the only one in the city

and this before the days of public pools—
but it was treacherous
even for boys his age.
Safe enough at first
moving through cool stretches
of small trees and bushes
in other places
it clung to the face of the cliff
and but a few feet wide
often sloped sharply across
in the direction of the downward side
only a loose steel cable pinned to the rock
to stop a sure slide to the edge
and over.

His mother took the challenge
not knowing the risk to her
and walked the path with him
down to the beach.
Before long he realized his error
and was terrified
holding himself between her
and a slip or fall
cautioning her about
this danger spot or that,
How they managed it safely
he never knew
but they returned to the Plains
by another way
and he was innocent of her terror
until back at the picnic
she told her friends about the path

shaking and trembling
as he looked silently on.

Of course she told his father
and he paid the price that summer
in sunny afternoons indoors
and in a cancelled day trip
to see his cousins in the country.
He had time and time again
to image in his mind that day
ending up as no picnic
and the Plains as no gentle place
of sandwiches and lemonade and play.
When he did go back to the beach
in the last days of August
he took the steep hill that everyone took
the one the cars went down in second gear
and his hankering for the rush and risk
of the Nanny Goat's Path
was tempered by the pictures he had made
during those days
when he'd stayed home, as his father said:
"to think about the foolery of your ways."

LEAVING THE COUNTRY

He'd been sitting there
for at least two hours
in the silent black
at the top of the stairs
outside the unlocked door
of his parents' second-floor flat
unable to walk in
fearful of his mother's scoldings
and his father's disappointment
and—when they found out—
his brothers' teasings.
He'd walked away that day
without telling anyone
from his father's cousin's place
in the country
just packed his cardboard suitcase
and left
at the quiet time after dinner:
over the gate—the one away from the house—
down the hill past the Powells' shanties
past the corner where his younger brother
was staying at their Uncle Frank's
then along the dusty stony road
and across the narrow bridge
at the rapids on the Jacques Cartier
—the Jack Carty his people called it—
and on to the crossroads
where the green Fournier bus

would some time that day show up
and take him home to the city.

He'd been sent to his Uncle Joe's now
—really his father's first cousin—
three summers running
for two weeks at a time
"to help with the hay."
And he'd taken well
to the work of the farm
learning the daily chores
and pleasing his uncle and aunt
who treated him as their own:
jetting the blue-white milk
pinging against the side of the pail
till it foamed over the lip
gathering the warm eggs
for breakfast
minutes after the laying
mastering the *tsk-tsk*
and the *gee* and the *haw*
and the *whoa-back.*
And the haying:
tramping down the load
as Joe forked up
stack after stack
till the wagon
was heaped over the top
and he rode high in the air
above the horse's back;
then the next morning

he outside walking the team
back and forth, back and forth
while Joe inside the barn
guided the pulley-riding fork-lifts of hay
high up and over
and into the loft.

There were moments too
scary for a small boy:
the time the four-foot-tall gobbler
took a run at him
when he got closer than he ought
and the black bull nose-ringed
lowering his horns his way
when he went for the cows
who'd wandered into the upper pasture
out of sight of the yard.

But it wasn't the long days
sweating it out on top of the hay wagon
or the gobbler
or even the fierce black bull
as much as the quiet and the dark:
endless idle afternoons when only
the chant of the cicada
and the mournful songs of birds
whose names he never learned
broke the absolute silence;
evenings lit with coal-oil lamps
falling away into black nights
devoid of any light.

So he'd left
three days into what was to be
a two-week stay
and now he sat there
thinking of what he would say
when his father told him
what he already know:
that they'd be worried sick
that they'd think he didn't like them.

Well he'd come back
and he was glad.
Summer was for the city
and it was his city
and he knew his neighbourhood
and beyond
upside down:
its every street and alley;
the Seven Hills
and the Plains of Abraham
and the Nanny Goat's Path
that led from there
to the beach at L'Anse au foulon;
the Citadel and the Terrace
and the *funiculaire* down to
Sous-le-fort Street;
and the long wooden stairs
down to Wolfe's Cove.
And most of all
he loved the city's life and light:
the streetcar bells from John Street;

the vegetable vendor and the ice man
yelling out their wares;
and the shouts of his friends
at hide-and-seek and stand-o;
and the glaring ceiling bulb
lighting his mother at her sewing
and his father straining for
every last line of Amos an' Andy on the radio;
and the street lamps
stealing the dark from the night.
And he was glad that he was back
and he would take the scoldings
and be happy.

After that
he went back to the country
on day visits with his parents
and later as a man
but it was years
before he stayed there overnight.
The times between
he'd spent mainly in cities
as if he needed that
to tell him he was not
—nor ever would be—a country boy.
When he did go back
the place was paved and lighted
and dotted with bungalows and splits.
Still he would have liked to think
that he could take it
now at least

but that was something that he'd never know
—and in fact for what?
for it was hardly a thing
to boast of
that the grown man might bear up
where the lonesome boy could not.

ST. PATRICK STREET, 1941

The slow fearful walk up Augustine hill
the side-long glances as he came to Patrick
then the dash across
and he was away free one more morning.

It had begun this way:
he had yelled one day for no reason at all
"Maudit pea-soupe"
at the huge raw-boned boy near twice his size
and run heart pounding
the other bright-red-haired and red-faced
in pursuit
till he was safe at Artillery and Michael
and well on his way to the Brothers' school.

Since then his mornings were a terror
till he got past Patrick.
He could have gone to school
by any number of other ways:
could have asked his Aunt Maggie
for three cents for the streetcar
could have walked along
by St. Matthew's Cemetary
any combination of streets and lanes
including short-cuts.
It was as if he sought the chance
to hurl his taunt again
and see the big fellow turn, flush
and lumber after him—

to flaunt his speed
in what would always be a failing chase.

He never saw him at the corner again
but for years Patrick never felt his feet
running or walking
but for that ten-stride crossing
on his way to school.
Though his father's cousins lived there
just a few houses from the corner
though the street was normal conduit
to church to skate to play
to many of his childhood destinations
he was a man before he ever made his way
along those two or three blocks of Patrick
where he knew the other lived.

They met again as older boys
at some awards night for their hockey teams
and he saw no recognition
in the other's eyes.
What he did see was their deep blue—
he already knew the flaming red hair.

Later still
he strove to make the pieces fit, the picture plain:
his own Irish side, the dread of St. Patrick Street
the lure of Saint Patrick's School
the other's Celtic roots—he was of Breton stock—
his own French lineage by his mother Grenier
the taunt, the chase, the want of grace
the fear, the shame, the pride, the blame

yet the parts stayed larger than the whole
and rendered but some flimsy shards of sense.
And no protests about boys being boys
or sure he was only a child
would ever drive the notion from his head
that something larger than the thing itself
lay there to be deciphered.

SWINGING THE BELLS

No doubting it at all
the sanctuary boys had it over
the choir boys when it came to
what you wanted to be:
you were up there with the priest
spouting off the Latin responses
swinging the censer
lighting the candles
ringing the bell
then breakfast with the Brother
in the back room of the sacristy:
all the toast you could eat
and three kinds of jam.

He'd been in the choir
three years now
and it was time to move up
but what sealed it for him
was the day after practice
they put them all into
black soutanes and white surplices
topped them up with
white celluloid collars and black bow-ties
and told them that
from then on they'd be parading
in their new attire
down the center aisle to the choir loft
before the high Mass on Sundays.

It wasn't so much the soutanes and surplices
or even the procession:
the kicker was the collars and bow-ties
that made them look like
the cherry-cheeked cherubs
on the Christmas cards
or *Les petits chanteurs*
who sang up at the Basilica.
From that day on
his *Kyries* and *Glorias*
and *Agnus Deis*
were half-hearted and weak
and the first chance he got
he asked Father Doyle
a priest who'd been at the house
if he could join the sanctuary boys.

He learned and memorized the responses
in no time
reciting them over and over
with his brother
and he knew all the actions
for low Mass and Benediction
after watching them it seemed for years
at a time when all the rituals
were set in stone:
when to change the Missal
ringing the bell—when and how many times
pouring the wine and water
raising the priest's chasuble at the Elevation
and all the genuflections.
When the time came to go on

he was ready
and the quiet awe and order
of it all
and the limelight he was in
caught and kept him
in their gentle grip.

But there were other things he remembered.
There was the time in the sacristy
garbed for Benediction
he nearly set his brother ablaze.
He was swinging the open censer
to get the coals glowing
when he struck Dan with it
and ignited his soutane
and the Brother saw it
and beat out the fire with his hands.
But the most fun they had
was swinging the bells.

Fifteen minutes before the 10:30
on Sundays
the church bells had to be rung—
as a rule the sexton's job.
One day, citing his occasional absence
the sexton showed them how
bringing them up to the drafty belfry
telling them which ropes to pull
how often to pull them
and how long to wait between tolls.
After pulling the rope down, he said
you must let it slide through your hands.

Some Sundays later
they were dispatched
up the steep stairs
past the choir loft
to do the job as they'd been shown.
At first they did it right
but soon one of them got it:
by pulling the rope down
then grabbing it
as far up as he could reach
he'd be lifted high into the belfry.
Before long they were all three of them
swinging about on the ropes
six feet off the floor
bounding from wall to wall
and pushing off each other
in a delirious melée of motion
not hearing nor caring
what this did to the sound of the bells.

That first Sunday nobody noticed—
or said they did.
The next time it happened
the Brother was in the belfry like a shot
chasing them back downstairs
and manning the three ropes two-handed himself.
After Mass he told them gently:
if you don't let the rope go
the hammer won't strike the bell
and come back—it won't ring right
it'll just ride around the rim of the bell
and what's more those old ropes are weak

and might break—and then what.
It worked for two or three Sundays
and they followed orders.
But Easter morning warm and sunny
Lent and winter both over and
the snow all gone
visions of huge chocolate eggs in their heads
and dizzy with fasting from midnight
they couldn't hold back.
He was the one to start
and then they were all swinging
and ascending and descending
in a grand ballet of fun and release.
This time it was the old Rector himself
who came up
fuming and ranting about putting your own pleasure
ahead of Our Lord's and the people's
banishing them all from the belfry
and him the ringleader from the sanctuary for good.

He never saw the inside
of the belfry again
though he was allowed in time
to come back and serve Mass.
It wasn't that he hadn't understood
that his own fun
had jarred the ears of others;
but try to do it
those ropes hanging there
like invitations to a spree
and his friends looking at him
just wishing for him to start.

For the rest of it: he'd missed
the early morning rush to Mass
the *Ad Deum qui laetificat*
launching him out
on his tripping dialogue with the priest
the smell of melting beeswax
the velvet chimes
skimming across the holy hush
at the Elevation
and his return
was life and breath to him.
But oh that yank of the rope
that took them up and out and away
on those swinging riotous rides;
that too was a gift—stolen perhaps—
but not soon to be forgotten.

A NIGHT AT THE CIRCUS

He'd heard the joke
more than a few times
and in different shapes;
the ten-year-old caught running
from the movie-and-vaudeville house
where he often sneaked in
through the back door
to watch whatever was playing
on the silver screen—
except that *this* day
he stayed to see
the live show in between
and got more than he could deal with.
"My mother told me,"
he told the burly doorman
who'd caught him rushing out,
"'If you ever look at a naked woman
you'll turn into stone'
and I've started turning into stone."

He remembered the story now
as he thought back to the April night
his pious old aunt
had taken him
hardly past his tenth year
to the old arena down town
to see his first circus.
Mainly it was a circus

like others he had seen in after years
as a boy and then with his own children:
clowns and jugglers and tumblers
trapeze artists and high-wire walkers
caged lions roaring and pawing
the tiger crouched on the elephant's back
then floating through the hoop of fire.
But it was not any of these
that marked the evening for him.

For as he lay in bed
later that soft spring night
his head was full of the one vision:
she had begun high in the rafters
and the rope extended
in a plumb line
nearly to the floor.
As she emerged slowly
from the pitch dark
into the circle of white
that bore her down
she began to shed her many veils
that floated to the floor
like wisps of tinted cloud
blue and purple and green.
By the time she passed him
at eye level
she was all but bare
her raven hair thrown back
her sequined breasts thrust upwards
one long leg extended out
and bent at the knee

back to where her arched foot
met the taut rope.
As she inched down
swinging gently side to side
the swelling and ebbing buzz
he'd heard all night
eased to a stillness
his aunt
who'd chattered cheerily throughout
was stunned to silence
and he sat rapt
not daring to move.

He'd often heard the older boys
he sometimes played with
whispering of their glimpses
of the dancers
through the back door ajar
of *Le Canadien* next to his house
or of their sneak-in visits
to *L'École des beaux-arts* down the street
where they'd seen the naked models
posing for the students in the studio.
But he'd never guessed
at the truth behind their whispers
and he knew now why they'd smiled so:
the pleasure that they'd had
was not just seeing what they'd seen.
Now he paid for his pleasure
for weeks
in nights sleeping and waking
heavy with close-up pictures

of a frowning God
till the gentle voice behind the screen
told him not to worry
that it was natural what he'd felt
and that God was not upset.

That lovely shocking woman
and her exhibition
was never mentioned by his aunt
not to him
nor it seemed to his parents
for the subject never surfaced;
it remained not so much their secret
as each's secret locked in each.
And his memories of that circus
were less of lions and tigers
clowns and jugglers
than of that languorous stunning slide.
That
and of the evening's finale:
the place was suddenly darkened
and as the crowd intoned
some grand melody of the day
(he never remembered which)
here and there around
spots of light began appearing
until ten thousand tiny flames
dispelled the blackness.
For a long time that circus
was for him but two scenes
all others pushed aside.
In later years he came to see

why this was so
or at least
why he himself
had made it so to be.

WAR GAMES

At nine years old or ten
war can be a wondrous thing
a continent away
its home-side apings
the delight of urchins
its local public face
the stuff to grace the lives
of carefree boys of play.

There were the sham battles
on the Seven Hills
of the Battlefields Park
to our excited eyes
more game than battle
more show than sham:
motorcycles flying from the crests of hills
to a bounding skidding landing
jeeps rolling up and down inclines
like toy cars on a playroom obstacle course
Bren-gun carriers spitting fake fire
grinding along through smoke screens
and the incessant popping of blank-shooting rifles.

Then there were the mock air raids
over the ancient city:
the sirens rising to a pitch
the rush to clear the streets
the lights-out

the looming droning Lancasters
the Hurricanes and Spitfires
cavorting in the sky
so low, we would say
you can see the pilots in the cockpits.
How we rued the all-clear
jolting us back to thoughts
of school or church or chores
the following day.

And the parades:
sailors in impeccable whites
bell bottoms slapping in unison;
crack commando units in khaki
putteed and helmeted and fierce;
air force men in blue-gray
all spit and polish and
fresh from the parade square.
And the brass bands
blaring out the marches
we heard and reheard
and carried in our memories
like the answers in the catechism
or the poems we learned by heart.

We were twelve or thirteen
when the shooting stopped.
One sun-washed summer evening
we watched mouths agape
as a huge troop ship in mid-river
leaning towards shore as if in yearning
was towed in broadside
by tiny tugboats

its land-side decks lined
with cheering soldiers from the war.
Yet for all the shouting and the joy
we were old enough to know
the ache of those who were not there
to greet them.
And the wonder of that night
was tempered by a new light
cast upon our merry days
of mock battles and parades.

FIELD DAY

He'd been waiting for it.
Still when Brother Mel
tapped him on the shoulder
that morning before school started
(it was grade six)
telling him:
"They want you for the track team
again this year"
so dubbing him pipsqueak knight
of the cinder track and sandpit
he was elated.
Last year he'd come out of nowhere
out of the shell of family
and a few friends
out of the winter and the snow
and the shrinking cold
—diminutive, bespectacled
the only one in his class with glasses
called *Four Eyes* and *Goggles*—
surprised them all
with gold ribbons
in the 50-yard dash and broad jump
and a red second place
with the St. Pat's relay team
at the interscholastic meet.

Now he could strut again
as he had that day

and build to another afternoon
of cheers and claps on the back
and the little boys pointing:
It's him! It's him!
and float home to his family
and for a day or two at least
be a hero in his own house.
So he trained with a will
with the others after class
and beyond that
sprinting back and forth to school
morning and afternoon
and at lunch time
uphill and down
and rain and shine
till they had to tell him
to slow down
or he'd run himself out of juice.

With the coaches
he was all ears and yeses:
running full belt at the board
timing it to strike it in the middle
with his right foot
launching him up and out
in an arc that was
neither too high nor too low
and making sure
to hit the sand upright
so his hands wouldn't fall back
and mark his landing short;
learning to get the baton

to the next runner
as close as he could to full speed
in the short space allowed
for the pass
carrying it in the right hand
and driving it up
—but not too hard—
between the stretched-wide
first finger and thumb
held backwards at hip level;
practising starts off the line
the cap gun driving them
from the mark
over and over
after they left too early or too late
then breasting the finish tape
at full speed with no let-up.

Came the day
and he was ready
in new high-top runners
and Bobby Wallace's
borrowed Paddy-green basketball shorts.
Three seconds into
the 50-yard dash
one then two boys from Garnier
whisked by him
and he finished in fourth place.
It happened again
in the relay
and to add to the disaster
he made a faulty pass

and his teammate dropped the stick.
He managed a third in the broad jump
but it was Garnier's day:
their year to strut
and that was that.

When he remembered the day
afterwards
he always thought of Charlie Ward
sitting high atop the sidecar
of the shiny white motorcycle
in soggy Quebec High shirt
—blue and gold slash shoulder to waist—
arms aloft
as the Plains of Abraham patrolman
drove him slowly down the cinder track
between rows of roaring admirers
then returning—after they thought
the patrolman had driven him home—
still perched aloft on the sidecar
a big Coke in one hand
a double-decker ice cream in the other.
Charlie Ward had that afternoon
won the pole vault:
leaving his rivals at ten feet
he'd had them raise the bar
first by two-inch gaps
then an inch at a time
clearing nearly every jump
on the first try
till he fell exhausted
after missing at somewhere

over twelve feet
all without the boon of
a plexiglass pole to spring him up and over
or a pile of foam cushions to take his fall.
By then the whole crowd was watching
and teammates and rivals both
—the Protestant Quebec High boys
and the *Jésuites'* Garnier boys
and the St. Pat's boys—
paraded him high on brawny shoulders
then delivered him to the patrolman
for his triumphal ride.

He never saw or heard of Charlie Ward again:
that burly smiling boy
habiting his mind
never changed.
Looking back on the day
it came as some surprise to him
that all the hopes *he'd* had
seemed to fall so easily by the way.
Was it that Charlie Ward's triumph
had softened his own dismay?
or had he just forgotten
over the years
that he himself had failed to win the day?
or was it that he's seen
in some inner kind of way
something beyond himself
larger than himself at play?

And what can you say
about a thing like this
but let the pleasure be
but let the moment stay.

CHRISTIAN BROTHERS

How gentle they were and firm
how kindly and stern
those brothers of our Christian school
Bonaventure, Hilary, Mel
in their black robes
and white rabats.
And how aptly did we
boys of the Depression
take from them
our rudiments, games, prayers.

Unmoved by the afternoon bell
he looked through the window
at ancient Abner
retired and late at his lunch
and marvelled at
the near-filled bushel basket
of red apples in the basement pantry.

Later, for a time
he took their name
and followed in their ways
and knew the sweet and tartness
of their nights and days.